D

67 Fast, easy and delicious dump cake recipes in 1 amazing dump cake recipe book

Table Of Contents

Dump Cake Recipes: 1
67 Fast, easy and delicious dump cake recipes in 1 amazing dump cake recipe book 1
Introduction 3
Chapter 1: What are Dump Cakes? 4
Chapter 2: Chocolate Dump Cakes 7
Chapter 3: Assorted Dump Cakes 17
Chapter 4: Seasonal Dump Cakes 28
Chapter 5: Berry & Cherry Dump Cakes 43
Chapter 6: Crockpot and Dutch Oven Dump Cakes 55
Conclusion 62

Introduction

I want to thank and congratulate you for downloading the book, *"Dump Cakes: Fast, Easy, and Delicious Desserts"*.

This eBook contains numerous tasty dump cake recipes that use common and inexpensive ingredients. Each recipe can be prepared in just 5 to 10 minutes and then baked for an hour. The entire process is simple and uncomplicated, even your kids can do it! Finally, no more slaving in the kitchen just to prepare a delicious dessert!

Feeling adventurous? Don't hesitate to experiment with other flavors using your favorite fruits and other ingredients. Use the various recipes in this ebook as your guide in creating your own signature dump cake flavor.

I hope you and your family will enjoy these dump cake recipes. Keep on baking!

Chapter 1: What are Dump Cakes?

Dump cake. The name sounds completely unappealing and even gross but did you know that this dessert is exceptionally tasty?

Dump cakes are typically made from a combination of instant cake mix, canned or fresh fruits, pie filling, nuts, chocolates, spices and other common and easy to find ingredients. These types of cakes are aptly called as such because all you need to do is dump your chosen ingredients in the baking dish and bake it. It is fast, easy, and very delicious! In fact, kids can make prepare their own dump cakes and just ask for adult supervision when handling the oven.

Just like other cakes, dump cakes are almost always fruity and very sweet. It is also made with lots of syrup, sugar, and butter so health-conscious people might get turned off by it. But nevertheless, they don't pass up the chance to taste a serving of these dump cakes.

Dump cakes are the favorite, hassle-free desserts in most homes today. Because of their versatility, the flavors that you can create are endless. No matter what ingredients you prefer to use, it will still come out crisp on the top, moist in the middle, and very flavorful. You can also enjoy it any way you want - warm, cold, plain, or with vanilla ice cream, caramel sauce, chocolate shavings, or whipped cream on top.

Before You Begin

No matter how easy dump cakes are to make, it won't be successful without the appropriate preparation. Here's how you can create delicious dump cakes without the hassle:

1. Read the recipes and check your pantry – In the mood of dump cakes? Browse the many recipes in this ebook

and choose a particular flavor. Once that's done, check your pantry if you have the appropriate ingredients needed to bake the cake. If not, opt for another dump cake flavor or shop for the missing ingredients first.

2. Follow the recipes – Some recipes call for cake mix preparation and baking before adding the ingredients. However, most recipes require the cake mix in its original dry form. Don't prepare the cake mix if it doesn't call for it, just dump it, powdered form and all, into the baking dish with the other ingredients.

3. Prepare your baking tools – Creating dump cakes isn't like rocket science. However, you still need the basic baking ingredients to make them. You'll need your measuring cups and spoons, spatula, spoon, fork, hand whisk, cutting board, butter knife, cooking spray, several bowls, oven mitts, and your baking dish. Some recipes may call for slicing fresh fruits, so a knife is also essential. A glass baking dish is very advantageous to use because it is easy to clean and often comes with a lid which makes storing leftovers a breeze.

4. Look the part – Whenever you cook something in the kitchen, it is always recommended that you wear an apron, wash your hands, and wear your long hair up. This is for hygienic purposes.

5. Cooking equipment – Dump cakes are typically cooked in the oven but it can also be made via a crockpot or Dutch oven. These cooking equipment have different controls and heat settings so be mindful of it. Some recipes also call for the use of a microwave or stove. If your child is making the dump cake, make sure to assist him/her during this step.

So are you ready to create your own delicious dump cakes? Just turn the page and go!

Chapter 2: Chocolate Dump Cakes

Choco Salted Caramel Dump Cake

Ingredients:

1 box devil's food cake mix, 1 package (3.9 ounces) instant chocolate pudding, 1 ½ cups caramels (chopped), 1 ½ cups cold milk, 1 cup semi-sweet chocolate chips, sea salt, whipped cream

Directions:

1. Preheat your oven to 350°F. Prepare a 9x13 inch pan by greasing it lightly.
2. Using a large bowl, combine the milk and chocolate bowl. Whisk well.
3. Put in the cake mix and whisk to combine the ingredients. Make sure there are no lumps.
4. Pour the batter into the pan and spread evenly.
5. Sprinkle the caramels on top of the batter.
6. Sprinkle sea salt according to taste. Don't put too much though!
7. Bake your cake for 35 to 40 minutes or until an inserted toothpick comes out clean. Remove from the oven and let cool.
8. Using a microwave-safe bowl, melt the chocolate chips on high for 3 minutes.
9. Spoon the melted chocolate all over the cake and serve with a huge dollop of whipped cream.

Easy Choco Pudding Dump Cake

Ingredients:

1 ½ cups cold milk, 1 ½ cups chocolate chips, 1 small pack chocolate pudding mix, and 1 box chocolate cake mix

Directions:

1. Preheat your over to 350°F. Lightly grease your 9x13 inch baking pan and set aside.
2. Put the milk in a mixing bowl and whisk in the cake and dry pudding mixes.
3. Pour into the prepared pan and spread evenly. Top the surface with chocolate chips.
4. Bake for 25 to 30 minutes or until the cake's edges ease away from the baking pan.

Classic Black Forest Dump Cake

Ingredients:

1 box chocolate cake mix, ¾ cup butter (sliced into thin pieces), 1 can (16.5 ounces) dark sweet cherries (pitted, undrained), 1 can (21 ounces) cherry pie filling, 1 cup walnuts (chopped)

Directions:

1. Preheat your oven to 375°F. Get a 9x13 inch baking pan and spray lightly with cooking spray. You may also opt to grease the pan with butter.
2. Pour the cherry pie filling into the dish. Add the cherries, with juice, and spread both ingredients evenly.
3. Sprinkle the chocolate cake mix all over the cherries.
4. Sprinkle the walnuts on top of the cake mix.

5. Place the butter slices all over the top, distributing evenly.

6. Bake in the oven for 40 to 45 minutes or until an inserted toothpick comes out clean.

Pineapple Black Forest Dump Cake

Ingredients:

1 box devil's food cake mix (select the brand without pudding), 1 can (21 ounces) cherry pie filling, 1 can crushed pineapple (18 ounces, drained but liquid reserved), ½ cup melted butter, 1 cup pecans (chopped), whipped cream, chocolate shavings

Directions:

1. Preheat your oven to 350°F. Next, prepare a 9x13 inch pan and lightly grease it.

2. Pour the drained crushed pineapple on the bottom of the pan and spread.

3. Add the cherry pie filling on top of the pineapple and spread evenly.

4. Sprinkle the dry cake mix all over.

5. Sprinkle the top of the mix with the chopped pecans.

6. In bowl, combine the pineapple liquid and melted butter. Stir well.

7. Drizzle the butter pineapple mixture all over the top of the cake.

8. Bake the cake for 30 to 40 minutes or until an inserted toothpick comes out clean. Remove from heat and let cool.

9. Serve the cooled cake with whipped cream and chocolate shavings on top.

Coco-Pine Black Forest Dump Cake

Ingredients:

1 box chocolate cake mix (divided into 2), 1 package (3.5 ounces) instant vanilla pudding mix, 1 can crushed pineapple (20 ounces, undrained), 1 can (21 ounces) cherry pie filling, 1 cup coconut flakes, and ½ cup butter (sliced into thin pieces)

Directions:

1. Preheat your oven to 350°F. Prepare a 9x13 inch pan, ungreased.
2. Spread the pineapple, juice included, evenly at the bottom of the pan.
3. Sprinkle the coconut flakes on top.
4. Sprinkle the first cake mix batch all over the pineapple and coconut, creating an even layer.
5. Next, pour the cherry filling on top and spread evenly.
6. Sprinkle the second batch of cake mix all over.
7. Distribute the butter slices all over the top of the cake.
8. Bake for 50 minutes to an hour or until an inserted toothpick comes out clean.
9. Let cool and serve.

Cherry Chocolate Cola Dump Cake

Ingredients:

1 box devil's food cake mix, 1 jar maraschino cherries (16 ounces, undrained and stems removed), 1 cup carbonated cola (any brand)

Directions:

1. Preheat your oven to 350°F. Prepare a 9x13 inch baking dish but don't grease it.
2. Pour the cherries, juice included, on the bottom of the dish. Spread evenly.
3. Using a mixing bowl, combine the cola and the cake mix.
4. Dump the cake batter on top of the cherries and spread evenly.
5. Bake for 35 to 40 minutes or until an inserted toothpick comes out clean. Remove from heat and let cool.
6. Enjoy!

Milky Crunch Pokey Dump Cake

Ingredients:

1 box chocolate mix (not the super moist kind), 1 jar (8 ounces) caramel sauce, 1 can (12 ounces) condensed milk, 6 Nestle Crunch chocolate bars (pounded into chunky bits), and 1 container (8 ounces)

Directions:

1. Preheat oven to 350°F. Prepare a 9x13 inch baking dish.
2. Prepare the cake mix and pour in the baking dish.
3. Bake according to package instructions.
4. Once the cake is done, remove from the oven and let cool.
5. Poke deep holes on the cake using the other end of a large wooden spoon. Make sure that the holes are in neat rows and columns and are about 1 ½ inches apart.
6. Pour the condensed milk all over the cake.

7. Next, pour the jar of caramel sauce all over the top.
8. Pour in the cool whip and spread evenly.
9. Sprinkle the chocolate bar chunks on top.
10. Put the cake in the fridge for 3 to 4 hours (or overnight).
11. Serve cold.

Yellow Chocolate Dump Cake

Ingredients:

1 package (5.9 ounces) instant chocolate pudding mix, 1 package yellow cake mix, 1 container (8 ounces) sour cream, 2/3 cup white sugar, 4 eggs (beaten), 1/3 cup water, 2/3 cup vegetable oil, 1 cup semisweet chocolate chips

Directions:

1. Preheat your oven to 350°F. Prepare a Bundt pan by greasing and flouring it lightly.
2. Using a mixing bowl, combine the pudding and yellow cake mixes. Add the oil, sugar, eggs, and water. Whisk well.
3. Fold in the chocolate chips and the sour cream.
4. Carefully transfer the batter into the Bundt pan.
5. Bake for 55 minutes or until an inserted toothpick comes out clean.
6. Let cool before serving.

Chocolate Marshmallow Dump Cake

Ingredients:

1 box chocolate cake mix, 1 ¼ cups water, 1 cup brown sugar, 2 cups chocolate chips, 2 cups marshmallow minis, 1 cup coconut flakes, ¼ cup butter, and 1 cup walnuts (chopped)

Directions:

1. Preheat your oven to 325°F. Prepare a 9x13 inch baking dish and grease it.
2. Prepare the cake mix according to package instructions. Set aside.
3. Put the water and butter in saucepan and simmer until the butter is completely melted. Remove from the heat.

    *When baking with kids or pressed for time, this can be done via a microwave.

4. Mix in the brown sugar into the water and butter mixture. Stir until the sugar dissolves.
5. Pour the sugar-butter-water mixture into the bottom of the pan. Carefully tilt the pan in multiple directions to coat the pan evenly.
6. Sprinkle the marshmallows all over the pan followed by the chocolate chips, coconut flakes, and chopped walnuts.
7. Pour the cake batter on top and spread evenly.
8. Bake the cake for 55 minutes to an hour minutes or until an inserted toothpick comes out clean. Let the cake cool for 10 minutes.
9. Put a cake dish over the top of the pan and flip the cake over. Carefully remove the baking dish.
10. Serve and enjoy!

Very Berry Chocolate Dump Cake

Ingredients:

1 box devil's food cake mix, 1 can (21 ounces) strawberry pie filling, 1 can (21 ounces) blueberry pie filling, ½ cup shredded coconut, ¼ cup walnuts (chopped), and ½ cup unsalted butter (sliced into thin pieces)

Directions:

1. Preheat your oven to 350°F. Prepare your 9x13 inch baking dish.
2. Pour the entire can of blueberry filling into the dish. Spread evenly.
3. Pour the strawberries over the blueberries and spread.
4. Sprinkle the dry cake mix over the fillings and even out using the back of the spoon.
5. Distribute the butter slices all over the top of the cake mix.
6. Sprinkle the chopped walnuts on top.
7. Bake for 40 minutes to an hour or until an inserted toothpick comes out clean.
8. Let cool and serve.

Strawberry Chocolate Decadent Dump Cake

Ingredients:

1 box Swiss chocolate cake mix, 1 can strawberry pie filling, 1 cup pecans (chopped), ¾ cups unsalted butter (cut into thin slices)

Directions:

1. Preheat your oven to 350°D. Prepare an ungreased 9x13 inch baking dish.
2. Pour the strawberry filling in the dish and spread evenly.
3. Sprinkle an even layer of the cake mix all over the strawberry filling.
4. Distribute the butter slices to the entire top of the cake mix.
5. Sprinkle the pecans on top of the cake mix.
6. Bake for 45 minutes to 1 hour or until an inserted toothpick comes out clean.

Chocolate Cherry-Orange Dump Cake

Ingredients:

1 box chocolate cake mix, 1 can (20 ounces) cherry pie filling, 1 can mandarin oranges (10 ounces, drained), 5 tablespoons unsalted butter (cut into thin slices)

Directions:

1. Preheat your oven to 325°F. Prepare an ungreased 9x13 inch baking.
2. Pour the cherry pie filling into the baking dish. Spread evenly.
3. Sprinkle an even layer of the chocolate mix on top of the cherries.
4. Arrange the oranges on top of the chocolate mix.
5. Distribute the butter slices on top of the chocolate mix.

6. Bake for 35 to 40 minutes or until an inserted toothpick comes out clean.

7. Serve warm.

Chapter 3: Assorted Dump Cakes

3 Fruit Dump Cake

Ingredients:

1 box classic yellow cake mix, 1 can sliced pears (15.25 ounces, drained), 1 can sliced peaches (15.25 ounces, drained), 1 can (21 ounces) apple pie filling, ¼ cup butter (cut into thin slices)

Directions:

1. Preheat your oven to 350°F. Lightly grease your 9x13 inch baking dish.
2. Pour the apple pie filling into the dish. Spread evenly.
3. Using a small bowl, combine the pears and peaches.
4. Use a butter knife to cut the fruit into smaller pieces.
5. Pour the combined fruits over the apple pie filling. Spread evenly.
6. Sprinkle an even layer of the cake mix over the fruits pieces.
7. Distribute the butter slices on the entire top of the cake mix.
8. Bake for 45 minutes to 1 hour or until an inserted toothpick comes out clean.
9. Serve warm.

Banana Dump Cake

Ingredients:

1 box yellow cake mix, 4 ripe bananas (sliced), ½ cup brown sugar, ½ teaspoon fresh lemon juice, ½ cup almonds (chopped), ½ cup butter (cut into thin slices) and whipped cream.

Directions:

1. Preheat your oven to 350°F. Light grease your 9x13 inch baking dish with cooking spray.
2. Arrange the banana slices at the bottom of the dish.
3. Drizzle the lemon juice all over the bananas.
4. Sprinkle an even layer of the brown sugar all over the bananas.
5. Sprinkle an even layer of the cake mix over the bananas.
6. Distribute the butter slices on the entire top of the cake mix.
7. Sprinkle the almonds on top.
8. Bake for 50 minutes to 1 hour or until an inserted toothpick comes out clean.
9. Serve warm with a dollop of whipped cream on top.

Banana Pecan Dump Cake

Ingredients:

1 box yellow cake, 1 cup pecans (chopped), 1 box instant banana pudding, 2 1/3 cups milk, and vanilla ice cream

Directions:

1. Preheat your oven to 350°F. Lightly grease your 9x13 inch baking dish.
2. Using a mixing bowl, combine the milk and banana pudding. Whisk well.

3. Add the box of cake mix and whisk until well combined.
4. Pour the batter into the baking dish.
5. Sprinkle the chopped pecans on top.
6. Bake for 40 to 45 minutes or until an inserted toothpick comes out clean.
7. Serve warm with a scoop of vanilla ice cream.

Fruit Cocktail Dump Cake

Ingredients:

1 box yellow cake mix, 1 small can crushed pineapple, 1 can fruit cocktail (21 ounces, drained), 1 cup shredded coconut, 1 cup margarine (melted), and 1 cup chopped pecans

Directions:

1. Preheat oven to 350°F. Grease a 9x13 inch baking dish.
2. Pour the fruit cocktail and pineapple in the dish. Mix well and spread evenly.
3. Prepare cake mix according to package instructions. Pour over the fruit layer.
4. Drizzle an even layer of the melted margarine on top.
5. Sprinkle with coconut and pecans on top.
6. Bake for 50 minutes to 1 hour or until an inserted toothpick comes out clean.
7. Let cool and serve.

Kiwi Orange Layered Dump Cake

Ingredients:

1 box lemon cake mix (divided into 2), 2 cups orange (seeds removed), 3 kiwis (peeled and sliced), ½ cup sugar, ½ cup

pecans (chopped), 1 cup butter (cut into thin slices, divided into 2), and whipped cream

Directions:

1. Preheat your oven to 350°F. Lightly grease a 9x13 inch baking dish.
2. Sprinkle half of the cake mix into the dish.
3. Place half of the butter slices top, spreading evenly.
4. Make a thick layer of kiwi and orange slices on top of the butter slices.
5. Sprinkle an even layer of the remaining half of the cake mix.
6. Put the remaining half of the butter slices on top of the cake mix.
7. Sprinkle the pecans on top of the butter.
8. Sprinkle the sugar all over the butter and pecans.
9. Bake for 50 minutes to 1 hour.
10. Serve slightly chilled with whipped cream on top.

Lemon Dump Cake

Ingredients:

1 pack (1 pound) angel food cake mix, 1 can (15.75 ounces) lemon pie filling, whipped cream and fresh strawberry slices

Directions:

1. Preheat your oven to 350°F and prepare an ungreased 9x13 inch baking dish.
2. Using a mixing bowl, combine the lemon pie filling and the cake mix. Stir well.

3. Pour the cake batter into the baking dish and spread evenly.
4. Bake for 20 minutes or until an inserted toothpick comes out clean.
5. Serve cool with cream and strawberry slices on top.

Lemon Cream Cheese Dump Cake

Ingredients:

1 box lemon cake mix, 3 eggs, 1 cup applesauce, juice and zest of 1 lemon, 1 cup powdered sugar, 2 packages (8 ounces each) softened cream cheese, and 1 teaspoon lemon extract

Directions:

11. Preheat your oven to 350°F. Lightly grease a 9x13 inch baking dish.
12. Using a mixing bowl, combine 1 egg, applesauce, lemon juice and zest, and the lemon cake mix. Whisk until smooth.
13. Pour the batter into the baking dish. Spread evenly and set aside.
14. Using another bowl, combine the softened cream cheese, sugar, lemon extract and two eggs. Whisk until smooth.
15. Pour over the cake batter and spread evenly.
16. Take a butter knife and make a deep (don't reach the bottom though) S strokes all over the cake. This will create beautiful swirls to incorporate the layers together.
17. Bake for 35 minutes or until the top is lightly golden.
18. Let cool and serve.

Lemon Gelatin Dump Cake with Lemon Frosting

Ingredients:

1 box yellow cake mix, 4 eggs, 1 package lemon gelatin, ¾ cup vegetable oil, ¾ cup water, juice of two lemons, 2 tablespoons melted butter, and 2 cups powdered sugar

Directions:

1. Preheat your oven to 350°F. Lightly spray your 9x13 inch baking dish with cooking spray.
2. Using a mixing bowl, combine the oil, water, eggs, cake mix, and gelatin. Whisk well.
3. Pour the batter into the baking dish.
4. Bake for 35 to 40 minutes or until an inserted toothpick comes out clean.
5. While waiting for your cake to cook, make the frosting. Combine the lemon juice, sugar, and butter in a bowl. Whisk well.
6. Drizzle all the frosting over the top cake while it is still hot.
7. Serve warm.

Mango & Cardamom Dump Cake

Ingredients:

1 box white cake mix, ½ cup mango puree, 2 large mangoes (peeled, seeded, and flesh chopped), ½ cup sugar, ½ cup pistachios (chopped), 1 tablespoon cardamom, and vanilla ice cream

Directions:

1. Preheat your oven to 350°F. Lightly grease a 9x13 inch baking dish with cooking spray.

2. Prepare the white cake mix according to instructions **BUT omit the oil** and use mango puree instead. If the recipe calls for 1 cup oil, use ½ cup of mango puree. Set the prepare cake mix aside.

3. Pour the chopped mango into the baking dish. Add the sugar and cardamom. Stir well. Spread the coated mangoes evenly on the bottom of the dish.

4. Pour the prepared cake mix over the mangoes. Spread evenly.

5. Sprinkle the pistachios on top.

6. Bake for 45 minutes to 1 hour or until an inserted toothpick comes out clean.

7. Let cool slightly and serve with vanilla ice cream on top.

Honey Mango Dump Cake

Ingredients:

1 box French vanilla cake mix, 2 cups chopped mangoes, ¼ cup raisins, ¼ cup almonds, ½ cup honey, ½ cup butter (cut into thin slices), and vanilla ice cream

Directions:

1. Preheat your oven to 350°F. Lightly coat your 9x13 inch baking dish with cooking spray.

2. Pour the chopped mangoes into the baking dish. Spread evenly.

3. Sprinkle an even layer of the cake mix over the mangoes.

4. Distribute the butter slices on the entire top of the cake mix.

5. In a bowl, combine the almonds, raisins, and honey. Stir to coat well.

6. Sprinkle the honeyed raisins and almonds over the butter.
7. Bake for 50 minutes or until an inserted toothpick comes out clean.
8. Serve warm with a scoop of vanilla ice cream on top.

Orange Dump Cake with Vanilla Frosting

Ingredients:

1 box orange cake mix, 1 package instant vanilla pudding, 1 package orange gelatin, 1 cup hot water, 1 cup milk, ½ teaspoon orange extract, 1 teaspoon vanilla, and 1 tub Cool Whip

Directions:

1. Bake the cake mix according to package instructions.
2. While the cake is almost done baking, combine the gelatin and hot water. Stir well to dissolve any lumps.
3. Once you take the cake out of the oven, pour the gelatin mixture all over the cake. Let cool.
4. Prepare the frosting by combining the milk, orange extract, vanilla, and vanilla pudding. Whisk until well incorporated. Fold in the Cool Whip and combine.
5. Once the cake is cool, spread the frosting all over the cake.
6. Put in the fridge for a few hours before serving.

Pine-Orange Dump Cake with Pineapple Frosting

Ingredients:

1 box yellow cake mix, 1 medium can mandarin oranges in syrup (undrained), 1 can crushed pineapples (20 ounces, undrained), 1 pack (3.5 ounces) instant vanilla pudding mix,

½ cup applesauce (unsweetened), 1 carton whipped topping (8 ounces, reduced fat variety), and 4 egg whites

Directions:

9. Preheat your oven to 350°F. Lightly coat your 9x13 inch baking dish with cooking spray.
10. Using a large mixing bowl, whisk the cake mix, egg whites, applesauce, and oranges together. Combine well.
11. Pour the batter into the dish. Spread evenly.
12. Bake for 25 to 30 minute or until an inserted toothpick comes out clean.
13. Let cool.
14. Prepare the frosting by combine the pudding and pineapple in a bowl. Fold in the whipped topping.
15. Spread all over the cooled cake.
16. Place the cake in the fridge for an hour or two before serving.

Pineapple Angel Dump Cake

Ingredients:

1 box angel food cake mix, 1 can crushed pineapple (20 ounces, undrained), and whipped cream

Directions:

1. Preheat your oven to 350°F. Prepare an ungreased 9x13 inch baking dish.
2. Using a mixing bowl, combine the cake mix and the crushed pineapple. Stir until well combined.
3. Pour the pineapple cake batter into the baking dish.

4. Bake for 30 to 35 minutes minute or until an inserted toothpick comes out clean.
5. Serve warm with a dollop of whipped cream on top.

Pineapple Carrot Dump Cake

Ingredients:

1 box carrot cake mix, 1 can crushed pineapple (20 ounces, undrained), ½ cup butter (softened), whipped cream

Directions:

1. Preheat your over to 350°F. Lightly grease your 9x13 inch baking dish with cooking spray.
2. Using a mixing bowl, combine cake mix, pineapple and butter. Stir until well blended.
3. Pour into the baking dish and spread evenly.
4. Bake for 40 minutes or until an inserted toothpick comes out clean.
5. Serve warm with a hefty dollop of whipped cream on top.

Pineapple Strawberry Dump Cake

Ingredients:

1 box white cake mix (the super moist variety), 1 can crushed pineapple (15 ounces, undrained), 1 can (15 ounces) strawberry pie filling, 1 can (3.5 ounces) shredded coconut, 1 cup butter (cut into thin slices, and whipped cream

Directions:

1. Preheat your oven to 350°F. Grease a 9x13 inch baking dish.

2. Pour the crushed pineapple, juice included, into the dish. Spread evenly.

3. Pour the strawberry pie filling over the pineapple and spread evenly.

4. Sprinkle an even layer of the dry cake mix over the strawberry filling.

5. Distribute the butter slices on the entire top of the cake mix.

6. Sprinkle an even layer of shredded coconut on top.

7. Bake for 45 minutes to 1 hour or until an inserted toothpick comes out clean.

8. Serve warm with a dollop of whipped cream on top.

Chapter 4: Seasonal Dump Cakes

Apple Pecan Dump Cake

Ingredients:

1 box butter golden cake mix, 2 cans (21 ounces each) apple pie filling, ¼ cup brown sugar, 1 cup unsalted butter (sliced into thin pieces), 1 cup pecans (chopped), and 1 ½ teaspoon ground cinnamon

Directions:

1. Preheat your oven to 350°F. Prepare an ungreased 9x13 inch baking dish.
2. Pour the apple pie filling in the baking dish and spread evenly.
3. Sprinkle an even layer of ground cinnamon all over the apples.
4. Sprinkle an even layer of brown sugar all over the cinnamon and apples.
5. Sprinkle the dry cake mix all over and spread it evenly.
6. Scatter the pecans on top.
7. Distribute the butter slices on the entire cake.
8. Bake for 45 minutes to 1 hour or until an inserted toothpick comes out clean. Let cool.
9. Serve with vanilla ice cream or whipped cream on top.

Apple Butterscotch Dump Cake

Ingredients:

1 box French vanilla cake mix, 2 cans apple pie filling, 1 cup butterscotch chips, vanilla ice cream

Directions:

1. Preheat your oven to 350°F. Prepare an ungreased 9x13 inch baking dish.
2. Pour the two cans of apple pie filling into the dish.
3. Sprinkle the butterscotch chips on top.
4. Sprinkle an even layer of the dry cake mix in top of the butterscotch chips.
5. Bake for 50 minute to 1 hour or until an inserted toothpick comes out clean.
6. Serve warm with a scoop of vanilla ice cream on top.

Apple Caramel Dump Cake

Ingredients:

1 box yellow cake mix, 2 cans (21 ounces) apple pie filling, ½ cup walnuts (chopped), ½ cup butter (sliced into thin pieces), caramel sauce, and vanilla ice cream

Directions:

1. Preheat your oven to 350°F. Grease a 9x13 inch baking dish.
2. Pour all the apple pie filling in the baking dish. Spread evenly.
3. Sprinkle the walnuts on top of the filling.
4. Drizzle the caramel all over the walnuts and filling. Put in as much as you want.
5. Sprinkle the cake mix all over the caramel. Make sure to distribute it evenly.

6. Distribute the butter slices on top of the cake mix. It is important to cover the entire top of the cake.

7. Bake for 30 to 40 minutes or until an inserted toothpick comes out clean.

8. Serve slightly warm with a scoop of vanilla ice cream on top and extra caramel sauce.

Cheesy Apple Dump Cake

Ingredients:

1 box vanilla cake mix, 2 apples (peeled, cored, seeded, and sliced), 1 cup cottage cheese (crushed), ½ cup almonds (chopped), ½ cup sugar, 1/2 cup butter (cut into thin slices), and caramel sauce

Directions:

1. Preheat your oven to 350°F. Light coat your 9x13 inch baking dish with cooking spray.

2. Arrange the apple slices on the bottom of the dish.

3. Sprinkle the crushed cheese over the apples.

4. Sprinkle an even layer of the cake mix on top of the cottage cheese.

5. Distribute the butter slices on the entire top of the cake mix.

6. Sprinkle the almonds on top of the cake mix.

7. Sprinkle the sugar over the almonds.

8. Bake for 55 minutes to 1 hour or until an inserted toothpick comes out clean.

Spiced Apple Dump Cake

Ingredients:

1 box spice cake mix, 2 cans (21 ounce each) apple pie filling, 1 teaspoon ground cinnamon, 1 tablespoon white sugar, 1 teaspoon ground nutmeg, 1/8 teaspoon ground allspice, 1 cup walnuts (chopped), and ¾ cups unsalted butter (cut into thin slices)

Directions:

1. Preheat your oven to 350°F. Prepare an ungreased 9x13 inch baking dish.
2. Pour the cans of apple pie filling into the dish. Spread evenly.
3. In small bowl, combine the nutmeg, cinnamon, allspice and sugar. Stir to mix well.
4. Sprinkle the spice mixture all over the filling.
5. Sprinkle an even layer of the dry cake mix all over the filling.
6. Distribute the butter slices on the entire top of the cake mix.
7. Sprinkle the walnuts all over the cake mix.
8. Bake for 50 minutes to 1 hour or until an inserted toothpick comes out clean.

Apple Caramel Dump Cake with Spiced Cream

Ingredients:

1 box yellow cake mix, 2 cans apple pie filling, 1 teaspoon lemon juice, ¼ cup caramel sauce, ½ teaspoon + ¾ teaspoon cinnamon, 1 cup melted butter, 1 cup heavy cream, ½ cup pecans (chopped), 1 teaspoon vanilla, 4 tablespoons powdered sugar and vanilla ice cream

Directions:

1. Preheat your oven to 350°F. Light coat your 9x13 inch baking dish with cooking spray.
2. Pour the apple pie filling, lemon juice, cinnamon, and caramel sauce in the dish. Stir well and spread evenly.
3. Sprinkle the dry cake mix on top of the filling.
4. Drizzle the melted butter all over the top of the cake mix.
5. Bake for 35 to 40 minutes or until an inserted toothpick comes out clean.
6. While the cake is almost done, prepare the spiced cream.
7. Using a cold glass or metal mixing bowl, put in the heavy cream and whisk until soft peaks are formed.
8. Mix in the vanilla, powdered sugar, and cinnamon. Whisk until well-combined.
9. Let the cake cool.
10. Serve with a hefty dollop of spiced cream on top.

Grandma's Apple Dump Cake

Ingredients: 1 box white cake mix, 4 teaspoons ground cinnamon, 4 cups Granny Smith apples (peeled and sliced), 1 cup apple juice, ¼ cup unsalted butter (sliced into thin pieces), ¾ cups brown sugar, and whipped cream

Directions:

1. Preheat your oven to 350°F. Prepare your 9x13 inch baking dish and grease it with butter.
2. Using a bowl, combine the cinnamon and apple slices. Make sure that all slices are coated.

3. Pour the apples in the baking dish and spread them out evenly.

4. Pour the apple juice all over the cinnamon-coated apples.

5. Sprinkle the cake mix evenly all over the apples. Smooth out using the back of the spoon.

6. Distribute the slices of butter all over the top of the cake.

7. Sprinkle the cake with brown sugar.

8. Bake for 40 minutes to 1 hour or until an inserted toothpick comes out clean.

9. Serve warm with a dollop of whipped cream on top.

Cranberry Apple Dump Cake

Ingredients:

1 box yellow cake mix, 1 can (21 ounce) apple pie filling, 1 can (16 ounces) whole cranberries, ½ cup almonds, ½ cup unsalted butter (cut into thin slices)

Directions:

1. Preheat your oven to 325°F. Prepare an ungreased 9x13 inch baking dish.

2. Pour the cranberries into the baking dish. Spread evenly.

3. Pour the apple pie filling over the cranberries and spread evenly.

4. Sprinkle an even level of the dry cake mix over the apple filling.

5. Distribute the butter slices on the entire top of the cake mix.

6. Sprinkle the nuts on top.

7. Bake for 1 hour and 15 minutes or until an inserted toothpick comes out clean.

Gingerbread Apple Dump Cake

Ingredients:

1 box gingerbread cake mix, 1 cans (21 ounces each) apple pie filling, ½ cup + 2 tablespoons unsalted butter (cut into thin slices), and whipped cream

Directions:

1. Preheat oven to 350°F. Prepare an ungreased 9x13 inch baking dish.

2. Pour the cans of apple pie filling into the dish. Spread evenly.

3. Sprinkle the cake mix evenly on the apple pie filling.

4. Distribute the butter slices on top of the cake mix.

5. Bake for 50 minutes to 1 hour or until an inserted toothpick comes out clean.

6. Serve warm with a hefty dollop of whipped cream on top.

Apple Dump Cake with Cream Cheese Frosting

Ingredients:

1 can (21 ounces) apple pie filling, 2 cups all-purpose flour, 2 cups granulated sugar, 2 cups powdered sugar, 2 eggs, 1 cup softened butter (divided), 1/3 cup softened cream cheese, 1 cup walnuts (chopped), 1 teaspoon baking soda, 2 teaspoons vanilla extract (divided), 1 teaspoon ground cinnamon, and ½ teaspoon salt

Directions:

1. Preheat your oven to 350°F. Grease and flour a 9x13 inch baking dish.
2. In a large bowl, combine the eggs, walnuts, flour, ½ cup softened butter, baking soda, cinnamon, salt, 1 teaspoon vanilla extract and apple pie filling. Stir well.
3. Pour the batter into the dish and spread evenly.
4. Bake for 1 hour or until an inserted toothpick comes out clean. Remove from the oven and let cool.
5. Prepare the frosting by combining ½ cup softened butter, 1 teaspoon vanilla extract, powdered sugar, and softened cream cheese. Whisk until fluffy.
6. Spread all over the cooled cake. Serve immediately or let chill for a few hours before consuming.

Apricot Dump Cake

Ingredients:

1 box vanilla cake mix, 1 pound fresh apricots (pitted and sliced thinly), 1 can (12 ounces) evaporated milk, 3 eggs, 1 cup

sugar, 1 ¼ cups melted butter, 1 teaspoon cinnamon, ¾ cup apricot fruit spread, and whipped cream

Directions:

1. Preheat oven to 350°F. Grease a 9x13 inch baking dish.
2. In a bowl, combine the apricots and sugar. Make sure the apricots are fully coated.
3. In another bowl, combine the eggs, milk, and cinnamon. Whisk well.
4. Pour the milk mixture into the bowl with the apricots. Stir well to combine.
5. Pour the apricot mixture into the baking dish and spread evenly.
6. Sprinkle an even layer of the dry cake mix over the apricots.
7. Pour the melted butter on top of the cake mix.
8. Bake for 50 minutes to 1 hour or until an inserted toothpick comes out clean. Let the cake cool.
9. Place the apricot spread in the microwave and heat until warm.
10. Spread the apricot spread on top of the cake.
11. Serve with a dollop of whipped cream.

Peach Coconut Dump Cake

Ingredients:

1 box yellow cake mix, 1 cup coconut flakes, 1 can (29 ounces) peaches in syrup, 1 cup pecans (chopped), ½ cup white sugar, ½ cup brown sugar, ½ cup butter (cut into thin slices),1 teaspoon vanilla extract, and 1 ½ teaspoon cinnamon

Directions:

1. Preheat your oven to 350°F. Prepare an ungreased 9x13 inch baking dish.
2. Pour the peaches into the dish. Cut the fruit pieces into smaller chunks using a fork. Spread evenly.
3. Drizzle the vanilla extract all over the peaches.
4. Using another bowl, combine the sugars and cinnamon together. Mix well.
5. Sprinkle the cinnamon mixture over the peaches.
6. Sprinkle an even layer of the dry cake mix all over the peaches.
7. Distribute the butter slices on the entire top of the cake mix.
8. Sprinkle the pecans on top of the cake mix.
9. Sprinkle the coconut flakes on top of the cake.
10. Bake for 45 minutes to 1 hour or until an inserted toothpick comes out clean.
11. Serve warm or cold.

Peach Butter Pecan Dump Cake

Ingredients:

1 box butter pecan cake mix, 1 can peaches in syrup (29 ounces, undrained), 1 cup pecans (chopped), 1 cup coconut flakes, 1 cup melted butter

Directions:

1. Preheat oven to 350°F. Prepare an ungreased 9x13 inch baking dish.
2. Pour the peaches into the dish. Slightly flatten with a fork.
3. Sprinkle an even layer of the dry cake mix over the peaches.
4. Sprinkle the pecans all over the cake mix.
5. Drizzle the melted butter on the entire top of the cake.
6. Bake for 45 to 55 minutes or until an inserted toothpick comes out clean.
7. Serve warm.

Peach Pineapple Dump Cake

Ingredients:

1 box yellow cake mix, 1 can (21 ounces) peach pie filling, 1 can crushed pineapple (21 ounces, undrained), 1 cup walnuts (chopped), and 1 cup unsalted butter (cut into thin slices)

Directions:

1. Preheat your oven to 350°F. Prepared an ungreased 9x13 inch baking dish.
2. Pour the crush pineapple into the dish and spread evenly.
3. Pour the peach pie filling and spread evenly over the pineapple.
4. Sprinkle an even layer of the dry cake mix all over the peach.

5. Distribute the butter pieces on the entire top of the cake mix.
6. Sprinkle the walnuts over the cake mix.
7. Bake for 45 minutes to 1 hour or until an inserted toothpick comes out clean.
8. Serve warm or cold.

Fresh Peach & Plum Dump Cake

Ingredients:

1 box yellow cake mix, 3 fresh plums (chopped), 6 fresh peaches (chopped), ½ teaspoon nutmeg, ½ tablespoon cinnamon, ½ cup butter (cut into thin slices)

Directions:

1. Preheat your oven to 350°F. Prepare an ungreased 9x13 baking dish.
2. Pour the chopped peaches and plums into the dish.
3. Sprinkle the fruits with cinnamon and nutmeg. Mix well to coat the fruits fully.
4. Spread the fruits well on the bottom of the dish.
5. Sprinkle an even layer of the dry cake mix on top of the fruits.
6. Distribute the butter slices on the entire top of the cake mix.
7. Bake for 45 minutes to 1 hour or until an inserted toothpick comes out clean.
8. Serve warm or chilled.

Peach Cobbler Dump Cake

Ingredients:

1 box yellow cake mix, 2 cans peaches in syrup (16 ounces each, undrained), ½ teaspoon ground cinnamon, ½ cup butter (cut into thin slices), vanilla ice cream

Directions:

1. Preheat your oven to 375°F. Prepare an ungreased 9x13 inch baking dish.
2. Pour the canned peaches, syrup included, into the can. Spread evenly. If you prefer, you may mash the peaches slightly just to flatten them a bit.
3. Pour the dry cake mix all over the peaches. Press down the mix firmly with a back of a spoon.
4. Sprinkle with cinnamon on top.
5. Bake for 45 minutes or until an inserted toothpick comes out clean.
6. Serve warm with a scoop of vanilla ice cream on top.

Peach Cherry Dump Cake

Ingredients:

1 box yellow cake mix, 1 can cherry pie filling, 1 can peach pie filling, ½ teaspoon cinnamon, ½ cup brown sugar, ½ cup butter (cut into thin slices), and vanilla ice cream

Directions:

1. Preheat your oven to 350°F. Prepare an ungreased baking dish.

2. Pour the peach and cherry fillings in the dish. Stir well.
3. Put in the sugar and cinnamon. Stir well to combine.
4. Spread the mixture evenly on the bottom of the dish.
5. Sprinkle an even layer of the dry cake mix on top.
6. Distribute the butter slices on the entire top of the cake.
7. Bake for 20 to 30 minutes or until an inserted toothpick comes out clean.
8. Serve warm with a scoop of vanilla ice cream on top.

Pumpkin Dump Cake

Ingredients:

1 box yellow cake mix, 1 can (12 ounces) evaporated milk, 1 can (29 ounces) pure pumpkin, 1 cup white sugar, 1 cup pecans (chopped), 3 eggs, 3 teaspoons cinnamon, ¾ cup melted butter, and vanilla ice cream

Directions:

1. Preheat your oven to 350°F. Grease and lightly flour a 9x13 inch baking dish.
2. Using a mixing bowl, combine the eggs, milk, pumpkin, cinnamon, and sugar. Whisk until completely blended.
3. Pour the pumpkin mixture into the baking dish and spread evenly.
4. Sprinkle the dry cake mix on top of the pumpkin. Create an even layer.
5. Sprinkle the pecans on top of the cake mix.
6. Drizzle the melted butter on top of the entire cake.
7. Bake for 45 to 50 minutes or until an inserted toothpick comes out clean.

8. Let cool slightly.

9. Serve with a scoop of vanilla ice cream on top.

Rhubarb Strawberry Dump Cake

Ingredients:

2 cups yellow cake mix, 4 cups rhubarb (chopped), 1 package strawberry gelatin, 1 cup sugar, 1/3 cup melted butter, and 1 cup water

Directions:

1. Preheat your oven to 350°F. Prepare an ungreased 9x13 inch baking dish.
2. Pour the rhubarb into the dish and spread evenly.
3. Sprinkle the sugar on top of the rhubard.
4. Sprinkle the gelatin mix.
5. Drizzle the water all over the gelatin mix.
6. Sprinkle the dry cake mix over the gelatin.
7. Drizzle the melted butter on top of the cake mix.
8. Bake for 50 minutes to 1 hour or until an inserted toothpick comes out clean.
9. Serve warm.

Chapter 5: Berry & Cherry Dump Cakes

Blueberry Peach Dump Cake

Ingredients:

1 box white cake mix, 2 can peaches in syrup (16 ounces each, undrained), 4 cups fresh (or frozen and thawed) blueberries, ¼ cup white sugar, 1 teaspoon ground cinnamon, 1 cup unsalted butter (sliced into thin pieces), and ½ cup pecans (chopped)

Directions:

1. Preheat your oven to 350°F. Prepare an ungreased 9x13 baking dish.
2. Pour the peaches and its syrup in the dish. Use a fork to mash the peaches in smaller chunks. Spread it evenly to cover the bottom of the dish.
3. Sprinkle the blueberries all over the peaches.
4. Sprinkle the cinnamon evenly over the blueberries.
5. Sprinkle the sugar all over the fruit fillings.

6. Sprinkle the dry cake mix all over the fruit fillings. Spread with the back of a spoon.
7. Cover the entire top of the cake with the slices of butter.
8. Bake for 45 minutes or until an inserted toothpick comes out clean.
9. Serve warm.

Blueberry Lemon Dump Cake

Ingredients:

1 box lemon cake mix, 1 can crushed pineapple (20 ounces, undrained), 1 can (21 ounces) blueberry pie filling, ¾ cup unsalted butter (sliced into thin pieces), whipped cream

Directions:

1. Preheat your oven to 350°F. Prepare an ungreased 9x13 inch baking dish.
2. Pour the pineapple and blueberry pie filling in the baking dish. Mix well and spread evenly at the bottom of the dish.
3. Sprinkle the dry cake mix evenly on top of the fruits.
4. Bake for 45 minutes to 1 hour or until an inserted toothpick comes out clean.
5. Serve warm with whipped cream on top

Crunchy Blueberry Dump Cake

Ingredients:

1 box yellow cake mix, 11 ounces fresh or frozen (and thawed) blueberries, 1 can crushed pineapple (20 ounces, undrained), ¾ cup sugar, 1 cup pecans (chopped), ½ cup + 1 tablespoon butter (melted), and vanilla ice cream

Directions:

1. Preheat your oven to 350°F. Grease your 9x13 inch baking dish.
2. Using a small bowl, combine the 1 tablespoon melted butter with the blueberries. Sprinkle the sugar by tablespoon and stir to coat the berries evenly.
3. Pour the pineapple, juice included, into the baking dish. Spread evenly.
4. Sprinkle the blueberries and sugar all over the pineapple.
5. Sprinkle the cake mix on top. Make sure that it is distributed evenly.
6. Drizzle the ½ cup melted butter on top of the cake mix.
7. Lastly, sprinkle the pecans all over.
8. Bake for 45 to 55 minutes or until an inserted toothpick comes out clean.
9. Serve with a dollop of whipped cream or vanilla ice cream on top.

Blueberry Apple Dump Cake

Ingredients:

1 pack white cake mix, 4 cups fresh (or frozen and thawed) blueberries, 1 can (21 ounces) apple pie filling, ¼ cup white sugar, ½ cup pecans, 1 teaspoon ground cinnamon, and 1 cup unsalted butter (sliced into thin pieces)

Directions:

1. Preheat your oven to 350°F. Prepare an ungreased 9x13 inch baking dish.
2. Put the apple pie filling in the dish and spread evenly.
3. Sprinkle the blueberries on top of the filling.
4. Sprinkle the cinnamon over the blueberries.
5. Sprinkle the sugar over the cinnamon and blueberries.
6. Evenly distribute the dry cake mix over the blueberries.
7. Put the butter slices on the entire top of the cake.
8. Sprinkle the pecans on top.
9. Bake for 50 minutes to 1 hour or until an inserted toothpick comes out clean.
10. Serve warm.

Blueberry Pineapple Dump Cake

Ingredients:

1 box yellow cake mix, 1 can crushed pineapple (21 ounces, undrained), 4 cups fresh (or frozen and thawed) blueberries, 1 cup unsalted butter (cut into thin slices), 1 cup pecans (chopped)

Directions:

1. Preheat your oven to 350°F and prepare an ungreased 9x13 inch baking dish.
2. Pour the crushed pineapple, juice included, into the dish. Spread evenly.
3. Sprinkle the blueberries all over the pineapple.
4. Sprinkle the dry cake mix over the blueberries and pineapples.
5. Cover the entire top of the cake with the thin butter slices. Distribute evenly.
6. Sprinkle the pecans on top.
7. Bake for 45 minutes to 1 hour or until an inserted toothpick comes out clean.
8. Let cool and serve.

Cherry Dump Cake (From Scratch)

Ingredients:

2 cups all-purpose flour, 2 teaspoon baking powder, 1 can (21 ounces) cherry pie filling, 1 ¼ cups sugar, ½ cup butter (slightly melted), 2 eggs, 1 teaspoon vanilla extract, ½ teaspoon salt, 1 teaspoon grated lemon zest, and ice cream or whipped cream.

Directions:

1. Preheat your oven to 350°F. Grease and flour your 9x13 inch baking dish.
2. Pour the cherry pie filling in the dish. Spread evenly. Set aside.
3. Using a food processor, put in the baking powder, flour, eggs, sugar, butter, lemon zest, salt, and vanilla. Process until well-combined.
4. Sprinkle the flour mixture on top of the cherry filling.
5. Bake for 55 minutes to an hour or until an inserted toothpick comes out clean.
6. Serve with a dollop of ice cream or whipped cream on top.

Cherry Pineapple Dump Cake

Ingredients: 1 box white cake mix, 1 can crushed pineapple (15 ounces, undrained), 1 can (21 ounces) cherry pie filling, ¼ cup butter, ½ cup margarine, and whipped cream

Directions:

1. Preheat your oven to 350°F and prepare an ungreased 9x13 baking dish.
2. Pour the cherry pie filling and crushed pineapple together in the dish. Stir well and spread evenly.
3. Sprinkle an even layer of the dry cake mix on top of the fruits.
4. Slice the butter and margarine to thin pieces and lay on top of the cake mix. Make sure the entire top is covered.
5. Bake for 45 minutes to 1 hour or until an inserted toothpick comes out clean.
6. Serve warm with a dollop of whipped cream on top.

Simple Raspberry Dump Cake

Ingredients:

1 box white cake mix, 1 package raspberry gelatin, 3 cups fresh (or frozen and thawed) raspberries, 1 ½ cups water, ½ cup sugar, ½ cup pecans, 1 cup unsalted butter (cut into thin slices), and whipped cream

1. Preheat your oven to 350°F. Prepare an ungreased 9x13 inch baking dish.
2. Pour the raspberries into the dish and spread evenly.
3. Sprinkle the sugar on the raspberries.
4. Sprinkle the gelatin over the raspberries.

5. Sprinkle an even layer of the cake mix over the raspberries.
6. Drizzle the water over the cake mix.
7. Distribute the butter slices on the entire top of the cake.
8. Sprinkle the pecans on top.
9. Bake for 45 minutes to 1 hour or until an inserted toothpick comes out clean.

Raspberry Lemon Dump Cake

Ingredients:

1 box lemon cake mix, 4 cups fresh (or frozen and thawed) raspberries, 1 package raspberry gelatin, 12 ounces lemon-lime diet soda, and ½ cup melted butter

Directions:

1. Preheat your oven to 350°F. Prepare a 9x13 inch baking dish and spray it with a light coating of cooking spray.
2. Pour the raspberries in the dish. Spread evenly.
3. Pour the diet soda over the raspberries.
4. Sprinkle an even layer of the dry gelatin mix over the raspberries.
5. Sprinkle the cake mix on top. Make an even layer.
6. Drizzle the melted butter all over the cake mix.
7. Bake for 45 minutes to 1 hour or until an inserted toothpick comes out clean.
8. Serve warm.

Raspberry Apple Dump Cake

Ingredients:

1 box white cake mix, 1 can (10.5 ounces) raspberry pie filling, 1 can (21 ounces) apple pie filling and ½ cup melted butter

Directions:

1. Preheat your oven to 350°F. Prepare an ungreased 9x13 inch baking dish.
2. Pour the raspberry and apple pie fillings into the dish. Mix and spread evenly.
3. Sprinkle the cake mix over the fillings.
4. Drizzle the melted butter all over the cake mix.
5. Bake for 30 to 40 minutes or until an inserted toothpick comes out clean.
6. Serve warm.

Raspberry Peach Dump Cake

Ingredients:

1 box white cake mix, 1 box raspberry gelatin, 4 cups fresh(or frozen and thawed) raspberries, 2 peaches in heavy syrup cans (16 ounces each, undrained), ½ cup pecans, 1 cup unsalted butter (cut into thin slices), and whipped cream

Directions:

1. Preheat your oven to 350°F. Prepare an ungreased 9x13 inch baking dish.
2. Pour the peaches, syrup included, into the dish. Slice the peaches into smaller chunks. Spread evenly.
3. Sprinkle the raspberries over the peaches.
4. Sprinkle an even layer of the gelatin over the raspberries.
5. Sprinkle an even layer of the cake mix over the raspberries.
6. Distribute the butter slice on the entire top of the cake mix.
7. Sprinkle the pecans on top.
8. Bake for 45 minutes to 1 hour or until an inserted toothpick comes out clean.
9. Serve warm with a dollop of whipped cream on top.

Strawberry Dump Cake with Cream Frosting

*makes two cakes

Ingredients:

1 box white cake mix, 1 package (8 ounces) softened cream cheese, 1 teaspoon vanilla, 1 cup powdered sugar, 1 container (8 ounces) Cool Whip and fresh strawberry slices

Directions:

1. Prepare the cake mix as directed on the box. Divide the batter into two 8" cake pans. Bake according to package instructions. Let cool.
2. Prepare the cream frosting: Combine powdered sugar, vanilla, and cream cheese in a bowl. Mix until full incorporated. Fold in the Cool Whip.
3. Divide the frosting evenly and coat each of the cake.
4. Put the cake in the fridge for two hours.
5. Top each cake slice with strawberries before serving.

Strawberry Almond Dump Cake

Ingredients:

1 box vanilla cake mix, 2 cups fresh strawberries (hulled and sliced), ½ cup almonds (chopped), ½ cup sugar, and ¼ cup butter (cut into thin slices)

Directions:

1. Preheat your oven to 350°F. Grease a 9x13 inch baking dish by spraying it lightly with cooking spray.
2. Pour the fresh strawberry slices on the bottom of the pan. Arrange it in an even layer.
3. Prepare the cake mix according to package instructions.
4. Pour the prepared cake mix on top of the strawberries. Spread evenly.

5. Distribute the butter slices on entire top of the cake mix.
6. Sprinkle the chopped almonds and sugar on top.
7. Bake for 50 minutes to 1 hour or until an inserted toothpick comes out clean.
8. Let cool.

Chapter 6: Crockpot and Dutch Oven Dump Cakes

No oven? No problem! These easy to make dump cakes can be baked using a crockpot or a Dutch oven? If you have either one, you can surely make your very own dump cakes!

Note:

Some crockpots are labeled as slow cookers. But it is very important to know that crockpots and the traditional slow cookers are not the same. Here are some of their major differences:

- Crockpots have heating elements on the bottom and sides while the slow cookers only have heating elements on the bottom.
- Traditional slow cookers uses moist heat to cook the food but in an intermittent on-off manner. Although also using moist heat, crockpots continuously cook food at low temperatures.

Using traditional slow cookers to cook dump cakes is not effective as the filling and cake mix might not cook appropriately.

Crockpot Dump Cakes

Tropical Fruit Dump Cake

Ingredients:

1 box yellow cake mix, 2 cans (15 ounces each) tropical fruit salad (drained, liquid reserved), 1 cup butter (cut into thin slices), 2 teaspoons cornstarch, and ¼ packed brown sugar

Directions:

1. Prepare your 6 quart crockpot and lightly grease it with cooking spray.
2. Pour the can of fruit into the crockpot.
3. Pour ½ of the drained juices into the crockpot. Reserve the other half.
4. In a bowl, combine the remaining juice and cornstarch. Stir well to remove lumps.
5. Pour the cornstarch mixture into the crockpot. Stir well and spread evenly.
6. Sprinkle the brown sugar over the fruits.
7. Sprinkle the dry cake mix over the fruits. Make an even layer.
8. Put the butter slices on the entire top of the cake mix.
9. Cover the crockpot and cook on low for 3 hours.
10. Serve warm.

Pineapple Crockpot Dump Cake

Ingredients:

1 box yellow cake mix, 1 can crushed pineapple (undrained), 1 cup melted butter, 1 tablespoon sugar, and vanilla ice cream

Directions:

1. Pour the crushed pineapple, juices include, into the crockpot. Spread evenly.
2. Sprinkle the sugar on the pineapple.

3. Sprinkle an even layer of dry cake mix on top of the pineapple.
4. Drizzle the melted butter on top of the cake mix.
5. Cover the crockpot and cook on high for 2 hours.
6. Serve warm with a scoop of vanilla ice cream on top.

Blueberry Pineapple Crockpot Dump Cake

Ingredients:

1 box yellow cake mix, 1 can crushed pineapple (undrained), 2 cups fresh (or frozen and thawed) blueberries, and ½ cup stick butter (cut into thin slices)

Directions:

1. Pour the blueberries into the crockpot. Spread evenly.
2. Pour the pineapple on top of the blueberries.
3. Sprinkle an even layer of the cake mix on top of the fruits.
4. Distribute the butter slices on the entire top of the cake mix.
5. Cover the crockpot and cook on low for 2 to 3 hours.
6. Serve warm or cold.

White Chocolate Cherry Dump Cake

Ingredients:

1 box yellow cake mix, 1 can (21 ounces) cherry pie filling, 1 cup white chocolate chips, ½ cup melted butter, and vanilla ice cream

Directions:

Directions:

1. Spray the crockpot with a light coating of cooking spray.
2. Pour the cherry pie filling into the crockpot and spread evenly.
3. Sprinkle an even layer of the dry cake mix on top of the filling.
4. Drizzle the melted butter over the cake mix.
5. Sprinkle the white chocolate chips on top.
6. Cover the crockpot and cook for 2 to 3 hours on high.
7. Serve warm with a scoop of vanilla ice cream on top.

Dutch Oven Dump Cakes

Cherry Chocolate Dump Cake

Ingredients:

1 package chocolate cake mix, 1 can (20 ounces) cherry pie filling, and 1 can carbonated cola

Directions:

1. Line your 12" Dutch oven with aluminum foil or parchment paper.
2. Pour in the cake batter and the cola in the oven. Mix well to create a batter. Spread evenly at the bottom of the oven.
3. Pour the cherry pie filling into the open and spread evenly.

4. Cover the Dutch oven.

5. Place 12-15 lit charcoal briquettes around the base of the oven, 18 lit briquettes in a ring on top of the lid, and 6 lit ones on the center of the lid.

6. Bake for 35 to 45 minutes or until an inserted toothpick comes out clean.

7. Let cool and serve.

Chocolate Dump Cake

Ingredients:

1 box chocolate cake mix, 1 package instant chocolate pudding mix, 1 ½ cups chocolate sweets, and 1 ½ cups milk

Directions:

1. Line your 12" Dutch oven with aluminum foil or parchment paper.

2. Using a large bowl, combine the milk and the pudding together. Stir until thick.

3. Put in the chocolate cake mix into the bowl. Combine well.

4. Pour the cake batter into the Dutch oven and spread evenly at the bottom.

5. Sprinkle with chocolate chips.

6. Cover the Dutch oven.

7. Place 12 lit charcoal briquettes around the base of the oven, 18 lit briquettes in a ring on top of the lid, and 6 lit ones on the center of the lid.

8. Bake for 35 to 45 minutes or until an inserted toothpick comes out clean.

9. Let cool and serve.

Apple Spice Dump Cake

Ingredients:

1 box apple spice cake mix, 2 cans apple pie filling, 1/3 cup canola oil, 1 can lemon lime soda, 1 cup pecans, and ½ teaspoon ground cinnamon

Directions:

1. Line your 12" Dutch oven with aluminum foil or parchment paper.

2. Pour the cans of apple pie filling into the oven. Spread evenly at the bottom.

3. Sprinkle an even layer of the cake mix on top of the apple pie filling.

4. In a spiral pattern, pour the can of lemon lime soda on the cake mix.

5. Drizzle the canola oil on top of the cake mix.

6. Cover the Dutch oven.

7. Place 12 lit charcoal briquettes around the base of the oven, 18 lit briquettes in a ring on top of the lid, and 6 lit ones on the center of the lid.

8. Bake for 35 minutes or until an inserted toothpick comes out clean.

9. 20 minutes into baking, open the lid of the oven and sprinkle the pecans.

10. Let cool and serve.

Peach Orange Cobbler Dump Cake

Ingredients:

1 box yellow cake mix, 2 cans mandarin oranges (8 ounces each, drained), 2 cans peaches (30 ounces each, sliced and drained), ¾ cup brown sugar, 1 can orange sod, 1 ½ teaspoon ground cinnamon, and 4 tablespoons butter (cut into thin slices)

Directions:

1. Line your 12" Dutch oven with aluminum foil or parchment paper.
2. Pour the peaches and oranges in the Dutch oven. Stir well.
3. Sprinkle the cinnamon and mix. Spread the fruits evenly on the bottom of the oven.
4. Sprinkle the brown sugar on top of the fruits.
5. Sprinkle an even layer of the cake mix on top of the fruits.
6. Pour the orange soda on top of the cake mix in the spiral pattern.
7. Distribute the butter slices on the entire top of the cake mix.
8. Cover the Dutch oven.
9. Place 12 lit charcoal briquettes around the base of the oven, 18 lit briquettes in a ring on top of the lid, and 6 lit ones on the center of the lid.
10. Bake for 35 minutes or until an inserted toothpick comes out clean.
11. Serve warm or cold.

Conclusion

Don't forget to share these recipes to your friends and family! Or not! You can guard these recipes dearly and just continue to wow them with your dump cakes every occasion you can. It's your choice.

I hope you have and will always enjoy the various dump cake recipes for many years to come.